SPRAINS AND STRAINS

ELAINE LANDAU

Marshall Cavendish
Benchmark
New York

This publication represents the opinions and views of the author based on Elaine Landau's personal experience, knowledge, and research. The information in this book serves as a general guide only. The author and publisher have used their best efforts in preparing this book and disclaim liability rising directly and indirectly from the use and application of this book.

Other Marshall Cavendish Offices:
Marshall Cavendish International (Asia) Private Limited, 1 New Industrial Road, Singapore 536196 • Marshall Cavendish International (Thailand) Co Ltd. 253 Asoke, 12th Flr, Sukhumvit 21 Road, Klongtoey Nua, Wattana, Bangkok 10110, Thailand • Marshall Cavendish (Malaysia) Sdn Bhd, Times Subang, Lot 46, Subang Hi-Tech Industrial Park, Batu Tiga, 40000 Shah Alam, Selangor Darul Ehsan, Malaysia

Marshall Cavendish is a trademark of Times Publishing Limited
All websites were available and accurate when this book was sent to press.

Library of Congress Cataloging-in-Publication Data
Landau, Elaine.
Sprains and Strains / by Elaine Landau.
p. cm. — (Head-to-toe health)
Includes index.
Summary: "Provides basic information about the different types of sprains and strains the body can get"—Provided by publisher.
  ISBN 978-0-7614-4833-4
  1. Sprains—Juvenile literature. 2. Wounds and injuries—Juvenile literature. I. Title.
RD106L36 2010
617.1'7—dc22
2009030915

Editor: Joy Bean
Publisher: Michelle Bisson
Art Director: Anahid Hamparian
Series Designer: Alex Ferrari

Photo research by Candlepants Incorporated
Cover Photo: Radius Images / Alamy Images

The photographs in this book are used by permission and through the courtesy of: *Alamy Images:* Greg Wright, 5; Digital Vision, 14; PhotoAlto, 17; Corbis Super RF, 18; Aflo Foto Agency, 19; JupiterImages/ Brand X, 24. *Getty Images:* Andy Crawford and Steve Gorton, 7; Doug Armand, 9; 3D4Medical.com, 10; John Giustina, 13; Vedros & Associates, 21; John Kelly, 22; Joe McBride, 23; Peter Dazeley, 25.

Printed in Malaysia(T)
1 3 5 6 4 2

CONTENTS

OUCH!

Oh, no! You can't be late for school again! The school bus is outside, and it won't wait much longer. You grab your book bag and race out the door.

Halfway down the street, you trip. You try to keep your balance, but it doesn't work. Seconds later, you're flat on the pavement.

You try to get up, but you can't. Your ankle really hurts. You twisted it when you tripped. Now you can't stand on that leg.

Your mother saw what happened from the window. She comes outside to help you. You have to lean on her to stand up. She motions to the school bus to keep going. You won't be going to school today. You'll be going to the doctor instead.

Hopefully you haven't broken any bones. Your mother says that you probably just sprained your ankle. This can easily happen in a fall. You don't know much about sprains, but you have a feeling that you're going to know more soon.

◀ **When you hurry, it's easy to trip and fall. Sometimes a fall results in a sprain.**

If you're reading this book, you'll learn a lot more about sprains and strains. Both injuries often result from accidents at home and at school. They also might happen when you play sports.

This book will tell you what to do if you get a sprain or strain. You'll also learn tips on how to avoid these injuries. So read on—and stay safe!

DID YOU KNOW?

The ankle is the part of the body that people most often sprain. Ankle sprains usually happen when a person's foot turns inward as he or she runs, turns, or falls. Every day more than 25,000 people in the United States sprain an ankle.

WHAT HAPPENED TO ME?

Who can get a sprain or strain?

    A. someone who plays soccer, hockey, or baseball

    B. someone who likes to play on playground equipment

    C. a couch potato who sits and watches TV most of the time

    D. all of the above

Was your answer D? If so, you're right. Anyone can get a sprain or strain. Even couch potatoes can trip on the way to the kitchen for a snack.

Maybe you've had a sprain or strain, or maybe you know someone who has. But do you know what sprains and strains really are? Do you know the differences between them?

YOUR BODY'S FRAMEWORK

First you have to know a little bit about how your body is put together. Skeletons are not just bony characters on Halloween cards. You can't see it when you look in the mirror, but you've got a skeleton, too. Your skeleton is the framework of bones that supports the rest of your body.

Skeletons give us our human shape. Without your skeleton, you'd be a very large blob. Can you picture a jellyfish as big as you?

Your skeleton does more than just give you a shape. It helps you move around, too. **Joints** connect the bones in your skeleton. A joint is a place where two bones come together. Your joints let you turn, bend, run, and twist.

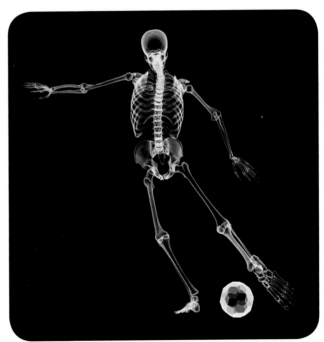

Your bones help you do lots of things. The bones in your leg and foot, along with your muscles, let you kick a soccer ball.

HOLDING IT TOGETHER

What holds your bones together at the joints? Scotch tape wouldn't do the trick. Cement wouldn't work, either. Instead, tough bands of tissue called **ligaments** hold your bones together at your joints.

Ligaments bend when you move. Without them you wouldn't be able to go anywhere. But don't expect them to stretch like rubber bands. If you overstretch or tear a ligament, you have a sprain.

A strain is different from a sprain. You get a strain if you overstretch or tear a muscle or **tendon**. Tendons are strong

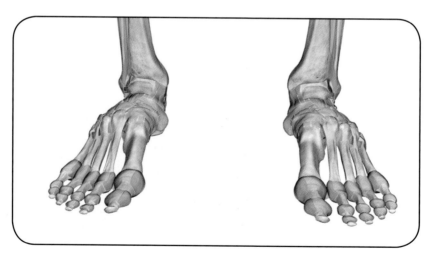

Ligaments bind the ends of your bones together. The word ligament comes from a Latin word that means a band or tie.

WHO IS MOST LIKELY TO GET A SPRAIN OR STRAIN?

How did you answer the question above?
Did you say, "An outstanding athlete?" That's not what
doctors say. The people most likely to get sprains
and strains share these characteristics:

- out of shape
- overweight
- have a history of pains and strains

Play it safe and stay in shape!

tissues that connect your muscles to your bones. Like sprains, strains happen when you put too much stress on a part of your body. Another term for a strain is a pulled muscle.

Many young people get strains when they play sports. Some strains are just a little bit uncomfortable, and they go away quickly. Others are more serious. One thing is sure—sprains and strains are no fun!

How It Happens

When you take good care of your body, it works like a super machine. It helps you lead an active life. You can play baseball, hike, dance, swim, and do other fun activities.

After an active day, you probably feel tired but happy. Sometimes, though, an injury can happen. You might end up with a sprain or strain.

OH, NO...HERE WE GO!

A sprain can happen if you fall down, make a sudden twist, or get hit by an object. Imagine that you're playing baseball. You need to reach first base, so you start running faster. You stretch your arm toward the base as you slide in headfirst. You make it before you're tagged, but you land on your hand. You go home with a sprained wrist.

Sprains can happen on the soccer field, too. As you kick the ball, you might land on the side of your foot. All of a sudden it's hard to walk off the field. You've sprained your ankle.

DIFFERENT TYPES OF STRAINS

Strains are common injuries for young people, too. Picture this: You're on the basketball court. Your teammate passes you the ball. You leap high to make the basket. You net the ball, but you don't feel the glory for long. Instead, you feel a sharp pain in the back of your thigh. You've strained your **hamstring muscle**.

Sometimes a strain happens as the result of

Playing by the rules of the game helps reduce sports injuries.

a single, sudden movement. Other times a strain can happen if you make the same movement over and over. For example,

THE STRAIN OF A BACKPACK

Do you have to bring home lots of books from school every day? If so, be careful! Wearing a heavy backpack can strain the muscles or sprain the ligaments supporting your spine. Put as little weight in your backpack as you can. Also, make sure to wear your backpack on both shoulders. Fix the straps so the bag's weight rests in the middle of your back—not too high or too low. Choose a backpack with wide, padded straps and a padded back. If possible, get a backpack with wheels.

if you typed at a computer all day for many months, you might strain your wrist. This happens because you used your wrist over and over in the same way.

Do you know people who play video games every day for hours without taking a break? Tell them that they are living dangerously. They could get a strain, too.

THE SIGNS OF SPRAINS AND STRAINS

How do you know if you've gotten a sprain or a strain? These injuries have some common **symptoms**, or signs. You might have a sprain if you notice pain, **swelling**, and bruising in a certain part of your body. Some people say they felt a pop or tear when the sprain happened. It will probably be difficult to move the sprained body part. For example, if you sprained your ankle, it will probably hurt to walk more than a few steps.

Strains cause pain and swelling, too. Your muscles might feel weak, or you might have **muscle spasms**. During a muscle spasm, the parts of a muscle squeeze together suddenly. It really hurts!

If you feel pain after an injury, never ignore it. Pain is your body's way of telling you that something is wrong. Get in the habit of "listening" to your body. Pay attention to its warnings.

WHAT TO DO

It's a hot July day. You go to the beach with your older brother. Your brother and some of his friends decide to play volleyball. You're excited because they let you play this time. Even though you are shorter than the older kids, you're a decent volleyball player. You want to show everyone that you're as good as the big kids.

The game is fast and exciting. You move quickly and jump high to block the ball. Your team is winning.

That's when it happens. As you leap for the ball again, you lose your balance. You fall and land on your right knee.

TREATMENT

You thought you heard a snapping sound when the injury happened. Now your knee hurts badly. Your brother has to help you to the car. You can't put your weight on the injured leg. It just hurts too much.

When something like this happens, it's important to act quickly. It's a good idea to start a four-step treatment plan called RICE. This is not the kind of rice you eat. Instead, the letters stand for what to do if you get a sprain or strain. This is how it works:

R = rest
I = ice
C = compression
E = elevate

REST

Rest the injured part of your body. For example, if you've hurt your wrist, don't try to play a video game. It's not the time to surf the Internet either. Your injury will not heal without rest.

Being careful can help you avoid sports injuries. Don't play sports when you're very tired or in pain.

If you've hurt your knee or ankle, try not to put any weight on it. You might need crutches or a **brace** for a while. It depends on how bad your injury is.

ICE

Place an ice pack on the injured area for twenty minutes, three or four times a day. If you don't have an ice pack, check your freezer. A package of frozen vegetables will do the trick. You can also use ice cubes in a plastic bag. Be sure to wrap the bag in a towel before putting it on the injured area.

An ankle injury can really hurt. Using ice and compression helps lessen the pain and swelling.

COMPRESSION

For this step, you should **compress**, or wrap, your injury with some type of elastic bandage. Wrapping the injured area this way keeps swelling down.

It also supports the injured body part and keeps it from moving around too much. Ask an adult to help you compress your injury. A doctor or nurse can tell you the type of bandage to get and how tight it should be.

ELEVATION

Keep the injured body part elevated, or raised. If possible, raise the injured area above your heart. Elevation helps prevent swelling, too.

Follow the RICE treatment plan for twenty-four to forty-eight hours after you get hurt. It might help to take **ibuprofen** to ease the pain, too. If

A young man elevates his foot following a sports injury.

your sprain or strain is mild, it may soon heal on its own. A strain usually takes about a week to heal, while a sprain can take about a month. You should start to feel better before that time. If you don't feel better, or if the swelling does not go down, see your doctor.

BE GOOD TO YOUR BODY

While you heal, try to take it easy. Get lots of rest and eat a healthy diet. Give your body a chance to get better. Before you know it, you'll be as good as new.

GET TO A DOCTOR!

See a doctor right away if one of these things happens:

- you have severe pain that continues after the injury happens
- you can't put any weight on the injured body part twenty-four hours after the injury happens
- there is redness in the injured area
- you think a bone may be broken or out of place

For a very serious sprain or strain, you might need surgery. An operation can repair torn ligaments, muscles, or tendons. Doctors called **orthopedic surgeons** usually perform these operations.

STAYING SPRAIN AND STRAIN FREE

When it comes to sprains and strains, it's better not to get injured at all than to have to work hard at getting well. Being careful really beats dealing with pain. Do you really want to spend time on the sidelines while everyone else has fun?

There are lots of things you can do to avoid sprains and strains. Here are just a few.

Do you like to go for walks or runs? If so, stay on flat surfaces.

Helmets protect bikers from head injuries.

Uneven pavement can be tricky. Many people trip on bumps or cracks and land headfirst.

Also, try to keep your room free of clutter. The same goes for stairs in your home. It's easy to trip over shoes, books, or toys.

DRESS FOR SUCCESS

When it comes to sports, dressing for success means wearing all the right protective gear. Do you like horseback riding? Don't forget to wear your helmet. Is soccer your favorite sport? Stay off the field unless you have your shin guards on. Do you live for skateboarding? Then be sure you're wearing knee guards, wrist guards, and elbow guards. Don't wear athletic shoes with worn-out treads or heels that are worn down on one side.

Wearing protective gear while playing sports helps prevent bruises, cuts, and broken bones.

Young team members do warm up stretches with their coach.

BE SAFETY MINDED ON THE FIELD

When playing sports, don't just rely on your body. Use your brain, too. Don't play when you are tired or if you're in pain. This will make you more likely to have accidents. If you already have an injury, you could make it worse.

Always warm up before working out. This helps stretch and prepare your muscles. Be sure to stretch the same muscles you're about to use. Cool down after exercising, too.

TIPS FOR STAYING SPRAIN AND STRAIN FREE

Try to exercise every day. That will keep you
in good shape. You'll be less likely to get hurt playing sports. Eat
a well-balanced diet, too. Eating healthful foods will help keep
your muscles, ligaments, and tendons strong. Finally, get plenty of
sleep. A well-rested person is less likely to have accidents.

VIDEO GAME INJURIES

You don't have to be on the field to get a strain. The constant playing of video games can cause injuries, too. Lots of kids play video games both at home and on portable game systems.

Sitting in the same position for hours is bad for your body. Using your thumb and finger muscles over and over also puts you at greater risk for muscle strain.

If you play video games, take lots of breaks. Try to keep your hands and wrists in a comfortable position. Also, don't play for more than several hours at a time.

You can't be sure that you'll never have a sprain or strain. But safety tips like these can lower the chances of injury. So play it safe, and enjoy your good health!

GLOSSARY

brace — Something that holds parts together to give them support.

compress — To squeeze or press together.

hamstring muscle — A muscle in the back of the thigh.

ibuprofen — A medicine that eases pain and reduces swelling.

joint — The movable or fixed place where two bones of a skeleton join.

ligaments — Tough, cordlike bands of tissue that hold bones together at joints.

muscle spasm — A quick, sudden squeezing together of muscle fibers.

orthopedic surgeons — Doctors who repair injuries to muscles and bones.

swelling — An increase in size.

symptoms — Signs of an illness or injury.

tendon — A strong tissue that connects a muscle to a bone.

FIND OUT MORE

BOOKS

Claybourne, Anna. *Healthy Eating: Diet and Nutrition*. Chicago: Heinemann Library, 2008.

Goodbody, Slim. *Avoiding Injuries*. Milwaukee, WI: Gareth Stevens Publications, 2007.

Miller, Edward. *The Monster Health Book*. New York: Holiday House, 2008.

Nelson, Robin. *Playing Safely*. Minneapolis, MN: Lerner Publications, 2005.

Olien, Rebecca. *The Muscular System*. Mankato, MN: Capstone, 2006.

Spilsbury, Louise. *Skeleton and Muscles*. Chicago: Heinemann Library, 2008.

DVDS

Healthy Habits 101: Teaching Kids to Stay Healthy for Life. Big Kids
  Productions, 2008.

Rockin' Rhythm Hip-Hop Kids DanceXercise. Nek-Nak Productions,
  2006.

WEBSITES

Kids Health

http://kidshealth.org/PageManager.jsp?dn=KidsHealth&lic=1&ps=307&c
  at_id=120&article_set=10321

Visit this helpful website to learn how to stay safe while playing sports.

University of Minnesota Children's Hospital

www.uofmchildrenshospital.org/kidshealth/article.aspx?artid=10514

Check out this site to learn more about strains and sprains. It shows
what to do if one of these injuries happens to you!

INDEX

Page numbers in **boldface** are illustrations.

ABOUT THE AUTHOR

Award-winning author Elaine Landau has written more than three hundred books for young readers. Many of them are on health and science topics.

Landau received a bachelor's degree in English and journalism from New York University and a master's degree in library and information science from Pratt Institute. You can visit her website at www.elainelandau.com.